# KICKED
## to the
# CURB

Where Policy Has Failed Our Most
Vulnerable Youth and the Fight for a Better
Tomorrow

By Susan Klinker Lockwood, Ed.D.

Publishing Services provided by Paper Raven Books

Printed in the United States of America

First Printing, 2018

Paperback ISBN= 978-1-7327694-0-3
Hardback ISBN= 978-1-7327694-1-0

To my parents,

who love me unconditionally

# TABLE OF CONTENTS

# ACKNOWLEDGEMENTS

I have wanted to write this book for a long time. At one point, after a long day advocating for kids, I remember hanging up the phone after a particularly frustrating conversation and saying out loud, "So once again, they get kicked to the curb." I wrote the words, "Kicked to the Curb" on a Post-it, and it stayed pinned to the wall of my office cubicle for the next three years.

Last year on my 55th birthday, my three daughters pushed me to get started writing. Had it not been for them, this book might still be in my head instead of your hands. Many thanks to Katie, Tricia, and Rebekah for challenging me to get it done.

Many thanks also to the very talented Patrick Posthauer for the fantastic cover design and my oldest daughter, Kathryn Lockwood Pesyna, for her detailed editing prior to my submission for publication. And I can't say enough about Morgan and her wonderful team at Paper Raven Books.

I am surrounded by a loving family and friends who encourage me and challenge me. I am blessed beyond measure.

# INTRODUCTION

When my oldest daughter was little, she used to look out our front window at the school bus stopped along our street, picking up the neighbor children. She would say, "Mommy, when can I ride the big yellow truck?" She knew there was something special about being old enough to go to school, and she looked forward to going there with the other children.

Similarly, I remember when I started kindergarten. My birthday was in the fall. Thanks to the state law in Indiana at the time, I had to wait an extra year before I was able to join the school crowd. So, when six-year-old me finally stepped foot into Mrs. Yoder's morning kindergarten class, it was safe to say I was excited. I don't remember much about kindergarten other than the walks home after school and the chocolate milk breaks during the morning. I remember cutting out paper dolls and gluing strips of paper together to make colorful chains to hang across the front of our classroom. School was a happy place.

I think about my experience with school in general. I remember I wanted to be smart, but I don't really know why. I remember I thought it was important to get good grades. I strived for straight As, but my dad always said, "Do your best, and that's all we can ask." My two older brothers were good at school, and I guess I thought I needed to be good at school, too. When I brought home a good report card, it was celebrated. At the end of the school year, a local hamburger franchise would reward an "A" on a report card with a free cheeseburger. My parents would always make a big deal of taking us there to recognize our achievements.

My parents were high school graduates. My father served an apprenticeship as a machinist for a railroad. We weren't well-to-do by any means, but we had what we needed. My parents sacrificed a great deal to send us to Catholic school. I remember my father working two jobs and my mother going to work outside the home when I reached middle school age. My parents instilled in us a value for education, and not only for my brothers. In my world, where Purdue University was practically in my backyard, there was never a question of whether I was going to attend college. My mother always told my younger sister and me that we needed to do something beyond high school. We needed to prepare ourselves in case something happened, and we were left to support a family. She said a college degree would provide us with more opportunities.

So, what's different about my experience and the experiences of so many others? Just like two people beginning a marriage don't start out by saying, "Yeah, we'll probably get divorced," I am convinced most little children don't show up at kindergarten on the first day and think, "I will probably drop out of school," or, "Surely, I am going to fail at this." They are excited about beginning. They want to learn and be with other children.

Yet, so many children never make it across the finish line 13 years later. The goal of achieving a high school diploma falls by the wayside. One of the factors influencing school dropout rates is the education level of the child's parents.[1] If the parent doesn't have a high school credential, there is a high chance the child also won't graduate. It's almost as if the children aren't expected to achieve. After a while, the newness and excitement of attending school is replaced by something else. Hopelessness takes the place of anticipation and expectation.

My parents made it clear to my siblings and me that school was a priority. "Do your best," was the mantra we heard all the time. When we did our best, it was celebrated. When

---

1 Child Trends Databank. (2015). *High school dropout rates*. Available at: https://www.childtrends.org/?indicators=high-school-dropout-rates.

we didn't do our best, we heard about it. They challenged us, encouraged us, and supported us. They were in the audience at my school plays and piano recitals. They showed up for my brothers' and sister's track meets and softball games.

Not only was school a priority, but our parents made us a priority. Were any one of us the center of the universe? Not hardly. But we knew we were loved unconditionally. To this day, my parents are my biggest cheerleaders.

Today, as with generations in the past, there are children who don't know what it is like to experience unconditional love. There are no adults challenging them in a positive way, rewarding their successes, or coaching them through hardships. There is a good chance the adults in the lives of these children are uneducated and unemployed. More than likely, these children live in poverty. Now, more than ever before, it is safe to say if these are children of color, their father is probably incarcerated or has been incarcerated. It is probable these children have witnessed or experienced violence, addiction, abuse, and crime. For these children, survival is the priority, not school.

Perhaps these children enter school feeling hope, but it doesn't take long for them to fall behind their peers. Life for them is incredibly difficult. The struggle becomes too much. Eventually, it may seem easier to drop out than persevere, because there is no one cheerleading them. Many of these dropouts become involved in the criminal justice system. They end up in juvenile detention centers and correctional facilities, where they are enrolled in school. As they encounter opportunities to find school success deep inside the system, they build confidence and begin to hope again.

Unfortunately, when they return to their communities, they aren't welcomed. They aren't supported. They usually don't re-enroll in school. Many unintended consequences from laws that were designed to keep them from being left behind prevent them from finishing school. Once again, it becomes easier to drop out than persevere. It shouldn't be that way. Youth need to have a level playing field. They shouldn't have to grow up too soon. They shouldn't have to work harder than their peers to get an education. They should be able to have the same opportunities to learn as everyone else.

Over the course of my career as a public school teacher and as a teacher and school administrator in juvenile justice settings, I have witnessed over and over youth who are getting kicked to the curb. Although they are usually viewed as difficult, there is more to their stories than what is seen on the surface. They have been kicked to the curb by the adults responsible for their well-being and a myriad of systems that allow them to remain invisible. At a very basic level, this population of youth who don't complete a high school credential become adults whose illiteracy costs taxpayers billions of dollars. More deeply, it raises moral questions about a society that allows its youth to be kicked to the curb.

*Chapter 1*

# NO CHILD LEFT BEHIND? EVERY STUDENT SUCCEEDS?

In January 2002, President George W. Bush signed No Child Left Behind (NCLB) into law, which updated the Elementary and Secondary Education Act. The law included an ambitious list of requirements setting the stage for increased standardized testing, specific guidelines for teacher licensing, graduation rates, school attendance, and overall school accountability. Because of this legislation, public schools were required to measure and demonstrate student proficiency in math, language arts, social studies, and science. Those schools not meeting the prescribed accountability measures were subject to a variety of consequences up to and including the replacement of existing administration and faculty.

The intent of NCLB was not a bad thing. Teachers and school administrators needed to make sure every child could read and do math at a proficient level prior to moving to the next grade level. In addition, the legislation attempted to close gaps in proficiency with children of color and children of poverty. Most people would nod their heads and say, "Sure. Makes sense." After all, if a person graduated from high school and couldn't read, write, and do math, that would be a problem, right?

Students needed to pass a standardized measure of proficiency in math and English if they were to earn a diploma. High school teachers often started testing students at the end of $10^{th}$ grade, so they could have subsequent chances to take and pass the test each semester of their junior or senior years (a total of five attempts) if they were unsuccessful on the first try. By 2011, the US Department of Education began requiring schools to report graduation rates in a standardized manner, measuring the percentage of youth who graduated within four years of starting the ninth grade.

This all seemed to be very reasonable. However, schools ran into lots of problems trying to meet the requirements of NCLB. First, the idea of using a standardized measure would be okay if we were measuring standardized children. But our children are not conveyer belt products. By the time some students finished the third grade, they'd completed two years of preschool, a year of kindergarten, and three years of elementary school. That's quite a bit of instruction leading to a test designed to measure reading and math proficiency. However, in Indiana, like other states, enrollment in kindergarten is not mandated. So, there were also students who had never been to preschool or kindergarten. They started first grade with none of the readiness skills their peers had acquired. To expect all students with varying levels of preparation to perform at a prescribed level by the end of third grade might not be as reasonable as first thought. All of a sudden, the reasonable had become very stressful.

Regarding school accountability, an Indiana law was passed requiring public school boards to base a percentage of teacher salary increases on student performance. This translated into teachers believing they could not get salary increases if their students didn't pass the standardized test. Or, if they taught subjects or grade levels that weren't part of the standardized test, they couldn't get salary increases if their students didn't meet specific learning objectives. This was very stressful for teachers, especially those teaching in locations with high poverty rates or with highly transient populations. Elaborate growth models and systems were put into place to provide some semblance of equity in measuring teacher performance, but at the end of the day there were teachers whose performance appraisals weren't as strongly impacted by the standardized tests as others.

To the public, a standardized measure was important. To them, it was an indicator of success. It was almost like quality control for schools or quality control for teachers. It reflected the quality of administrative leadership and the quality of teacher instruction. Your students can't pass the test? You must not be a very good teacher. Your school's overall percentage rate of students passing the test is below average? Your school must not be very good.

But to a child, passing or failing the standardized test meant he had either performed well enough, or he hadn't. To an eight-year-old third grader, not passing the test branded him a failure. To a 14- or 15-year-old algebra student, not passing the test meant he couldn't graduate.

As states did their best to meet the often-unfunded or underfunded requirements of NCLB, it became clear there were unintended consequences. Remediation was costly, and the NCLB legislation didn't exactly bring a lot of extra funding to school corporations. School administrators and teachers often complained about unfunded mandates, and state departments of education and state legislatures were met with significant budgeting issues.

The law provided states with leniency to excuse a portion of some student subgroups when it came to reporting scores from standardized tests. Naturally, many students identified for special education services fell into this category. However, some students didn't qualify for special education, yet couldn't demonstrate proficiency on the test. These children were problematic for schools who were not meeting performance measures. They impacted the school's accountability score in a negative way.

Another group that had a negative impact on school accountability scores were the transient students. These were the students who didn't stay in one school for an entire school year. To be clear, these weren't children whose parents relocated for a job and had to enroll in a new school once or twice over the course of a K–12 timeframe. These were children whose parents were dodging landlords, because they couldn't make rent. These were children who were jostled among foster homes or family members assigned to care for them due to an absent parent. These students, through no fault of their own, struggled to keep up with their peers because they were constantly changing schools. In Indiana, this issue of transience was addressed by looking at the number of days a student had been enrolled in the school at the time he took the test. If he hadn't attended the school for at least 160 days prior to taking the test, he wasn't included in the school's overall accountability score.

The intent of NCLB was good. Like its title, people were trying to assure that no child was left behind. However, there were many ways in which a student could remain uncounted when measuring school accountability. Public schools found ways to make sure various subgroups of the student population didn't have a negative impact on the final accountability score.

The students in these subgroups were the ones who typically ended up dropping out of school. They struggled academically and often behaviorally. In the end, they were either suspended, expelled, or they quit because they got tired of trying. So, now that this underachieving youth was no longer on the enrollment roster of the public school in Anywhere, USA, what happened to him? No Child Left Behind, later reauthorized as Every Student Succeeds, was meant for every child, right?

Not so fast. To be kept from being left behind, someone needs to notice you aren't there.

## Chapter 2
# WHAT'S "NORMAL"?

When I started teaching in the mid-1980s, I truly thought everyone who started school in kindergarten would graduate after 12th grade with a high school diploma. That was my normal. I knew there were programs to teach adults how to read, and I knew some people didn't finish high school and had to take the GED test, but I really had no grasp of the true reality of illiteracy. All the adults in my life had high school diplomas. Didn't everyone?

Before judging me, remember I was born and raised in the heart of the Midwest. At the time, there was not a lot of ethnic diversity in my world. The Midwest economy was based on agriculture and manufacturing. There was a cornfield behind my house and a soybean field across the street. My cousins lived next door. Although I am sure there must have been poverty in my community and my state, I wasn't around it very much. My school experience was successful and the students who went to school with me were successful. As a child and even as a high school student, my worldview was limited.

Growing up, I had zero experience with the criminal justice system, except for all those speeding tickets I racked up when I was an undergraduate college student. And later I was a music teacher, so I had students with special needs in my vocal music classes, but their learning or cognitive disabilities didn't interfere with their ability to succeed in my classroom.

One day, I received a message about a 15-year-old girl who I had known since she was in my seventh-grade choir. She had been arrested for murdering her mother. I was stunned. Just like that, I never saw her again. Her empty seat in my sixth period ninth-grade choir made me sad, but there was nothing I could do about it. A few days later, I was standing outside my classroom, chatting with a colleague, and commented about it. He was a longtime veteran teacher, and he casually stated, "Yes, you never know how many future felons are sitting right in front of you every day." Wow. Was he joking? Was I naïve? I didn't know how to respond. As the days went on, I wondered what could cause a 15-year-old to commit such a violent act, but it was so far outside of my normal I couldn't imagine her reality. After a while, I forgot about her.

Fast forward several years later to a different job teaching general music in an elementary school. At this school, students who were identified with special needs always came to music, art, and physical education classes. I taught at this school long enough to see two entire cohorts advance from kindergarten to completion of fifth grade. I enjoyed watching the children grow before my very eyes. Since I taught all grade levels in the school, I often had siblings in my classroom. I found parents of elementary school children tended to be more involved in the school. I often got to know them, especially when they had more than one child attending. The parents seemed to enjoy coming to the school and talking with teachers. The parents were highly supportive and the Parent Teacher Organization (PTO) sponsored many fundraising activities to purchase extra resources for classrooms. The school felt like an extension of the community where it was located, and people often talked about their school family.

While teaching at that school, I remember students who seemed to struggle, but one in particular stood out. As he progressed from kindergarten, he was identified to receive special education services. He often got into trouble in his classroom, and he was one of those students who would be found sitting at his desk in the hall, completing his work. At one point, I asked the special education teacher if there was anything I could do to help this student. After all, he was one of my students, too. She suggested I could be an adult who checked in with him at the beginning and ending of every day to see how he was doing. To me, that didn't seem like a big deal, so I agreed to do it. For the next two weeks, I checked in with him at the beginning and end of every day, and I noticed he started smiling more. He started participating during my class, and I didn't see him out in the hall as much. We continued our check-ins for several weeks and then, clear out of the blue, he was gone. I asked what happened to him and was told he had gone to live with another family member. I was sad because I had come to enjoy our daily chats, and I believed he enjoyed them, too. I didn't get the chance to say good-bye.

The student taught me something very important. Every person wants to be noticed. I wondered if he was tired of being the one who always got the answer wrong, or the one who was always causing trouble. For once, someone was stopping by every day simply to say hello, with no strings attached. Similarly, before he got on the bus, the same person would check to see he had his homework together for his book bag, wish him a good evening, and say, "See you tomorrow!" How many times had I stood in the hallway as students passed without genuinely saying "hello" as they walked past me? What if I took time to truly notice children and give them a smile as they headed towards their classrooms? Would it make a difference? Were there adults in their lives who did that for them as they left the house or arrived home from work? Maybe my normal wasn't the same as theirs.

This was the beginning of my career transition from music teacher to special education teacher. I loved teaching music, but I started to develop an even deeper passion for those children who seemed to be on the fringe of things. I thought about the students who were considered difficult. In other words, the students who caused trouble during class, who interrupted instruction, who never had their assignments completed, and who took so much of everyone's time. What caused them to behave the way they did?

It took me almost 20 years to realize I was asking the wrong question. Instead of "What causes you to behave the way you do?" I should have been asking myself, "What happened to you that causes you to behave this way?" Finally, I had learned children don't always come from home environments with nurturing adults and positive support. I had grown from knowing *about* these children to actually *knowing* these children. Their normal was very different than my normal.

Think about what it is like when you are at work and you get hungry. If you are lucky, you have a snack stashed away somewhere, or you can grab something from your locker or a vending machine. Even if a snack isn't in your near future, you probably had a meal before the start of your shift, and you know you will get to eat another one within the next hour or two. However, it doesn't matter. Right now, you are hungry. After a while, it gets hard to concentrate because all you can think about is your growling stomach. You keep watching the clock. Your productivity is low.

Think about a time you had a fight with your spouse or someone who lived with you. A lot of things were said, and you couldn't get them out of your mind. You might have lost sleep over it, because you worried about it so much. You may also have been frightened by some of the things said, and perhaps you felt your physical safety was threatened.

Speaking from experience, I know it is hard to concentrate on work when other things are on my mind. Sometimes I am hungry. Sometimes I am cold. Maybe I didn't get enough sleep prior to arriving at work. Maybe I am worrying about one of my children. However, I am an adult and I have learned strategies along the way to help me get back on track and do what I need to do. Children haven't learned strategies for getting back on track. It is hard for them to focus if they are hungry, if they didn't get enough sleep, or if they are worried about their safety or that of another family member. Like I said before, some children are more concerned with survival than education.

Their normal is not the same as mine.

*Chapter 3*

# THE REALITY OF TRAUMA

What do children experience outside of the school day when they are at home alone? I am not talking about latchkey children who come home from school to an empty house where there is no adult between the hours of 3 and 5PM. I am referring to those children who are basically on their own from the time they leave school until the next morning. There might be adults or babysitters present, but they aren't really involved. The children I'm describing don't have someone there who is taking a genuine interest in them. They often see adults abuse drugs or alcohol. They have probably been witness to criminal activity or personally experienced violent acts. These children are not sitting at the kitchen table doing homework while mom and dad supervise. They are alone in a house full of people. If there is food, they are probably making it for themselves and even for their younger siblings. They have learned to stay out of the way of the adults, who are either abusive to them or ignore them.

Naturally, this reality has a serious impact on children. Although the public school might be a safer place for them in the physical sense, they arrive at school with a lot on their minds. Can they trust the adults who are in the school? If they step out of line in any way, will they be physically punished? When an adult raises his voice at school, does it mean he will hurt them? Is it safe to trust the other children?

If a child is afraid for his safety at home, he is probably jittery at school as well. After all, the people at home are his normal. He has come to expect that he needs to behave in a certain way to survive. He might sit in his classroom feeling the need to look over his shoulder to make sure he is safe. Since he hasn't done any of his homework, he is probably falling behind his peers. Plus, he is experiencing the consequences of incomplete assignments and lower grades. There is little in his life over which he has any control.

It is not dramatic to say a lot of young people escape their home lives by hitting the streets. Staying away from home during the times when the adults are there is a survival mechanism. After all, no one at home is paying attention. Youths find friends on the street who recognize their vulnerability. Before long, they become entangled in situations as unhealthy as the ones they endured at home…alcohol, substance abuse, crime, and sometimes worse…sex trafficking, sexual and emotional abuse, or gangs. Going to school is the last thing on their radars; even if they manage to get to school, their attendance is sporadic. They struggle, because they are thinking about other things instead of focusing on learning.

There are many youths whose normal is far from normal; however, they know nothing else. They are caught in a cycle that seems to be unbreakable. It is a sad story, played out repeatedly, and seems very hopeless. Victims of trauma almost always go back to what they know, even if it is bad, because that's all they know.

Imagine what it would be like if you went to work every day and failed at most of the tasks you were assigned to do. Not only did you fail them, but your peers watched you fail. Your boss would try to be patient with you and give you extra help, but your peers would respond, "Unfair! I didn't get any special help!" You would go to lunch in the employee cafeteria and hear your peers talking about you and calling you names. How many days would you last in an environment such as this? Even if you remained, at some point your boss would probably get tired of spending so much time with you. He might even decide you were hopeless and terminate your employment.

Children who struggle in school deal with this type of environment every day. School is difficult for them. They have trouble finding success. Some are identified to receive special education services, which can bring about a stigma from being labeled. They encounter teachers who might not think it is fair to provide them with appropriate accommodations or are not aware they even need them. These students and their teachers are pressured to succeed because of the need for the school to meet its accountability measures. And yet, the deck appears to be stacked against them, because normal for these children doesn't align with the normal of the standardized test.

These young people are victims. They are at the mercy of the adults who brought them into the world and are supposed to be caring for them. Not only do these adults neglect the education of their children, they simply don't provide care for them. These young people might start school with excitement and anticipation, but it doesn't take long for them to fall behind their peers. With no one at home to encourage them, it is easier to drop out of school altogether than to go to a place every day where they are not successful. We need to level the playing field for our children. Opportunity is not equally distributed.

*Chapter 4*

# THE IMPACT OF LOW LITERACY AND NUMERACY SKILLS

According to statistics from ProLiteracy, an international nonprofit organization supporting programs helping adults learn to read and write, there are 36 million adults in the United States who are unable to read, write, or do basic math at the third-grade level.[2] Not only that, but of the adults with the lowest reading levels, 43 percent live in poverty. An adult who is marginally literate is typically unemployed; if he finds a job, his wages are likely lower than the national average.

2 Adult Literacy Facts. (2018) Available at: https://proliteracy.org/ Resources/Adult-Literacy-Facts

Again, according to ProLiteracy, low literacy and numeracy costs the United States at least $225 billion each year...*each year*...in non-productivity in the workforce, crime, and loss of tax revenue due to unemployment.[3] What a staggering statistic! Unfortunately, since most people don't know about the tremendous cost associated with low literacy and numeracy, there aren't many in our society who are advocating for legislatures to increase the resources to address it.

Data reflect one in six young adults drop out of high school each year.[4] Bringing it closer to home, I thought about six teenagers who were important to me, and which one of them I would allow to drop out of high school. Then, I thought about six more teenagers who were important to me and which one of them I would allow to drop out of high school the next year. Of course, I would do everything I could to make sure those 12 teenagers all stayed in school and made it across the finish line. One in six young adults dropping out of high school each year is a sobering statistic and scary to personalize.

What is the impact of all of this? When youth don't finish high school, the path to a high school credential is through adult education. Adult education programs are funded with state and federal tax dollars. However, the national average expenditure per adult learner is $800. By contrast, the average annual per-pupil expenditure on public elementary

---

3 Adult Literacy Facts. (2018) Available at: https://proliteracy.org/
Resources/Adult-Literacy-Facts
4 Adult Ed Facts. (2018) Available at https://www.worlded.org/
WEIInternet/us/adult-ed-facts.cfm

and secondary education is over $10,000. Adult education programs receive less than 10 percent of the amount of federal, state, and local funding going to K–12, and less than five percent of what is spent to support higher education.[5] When you consider how many school superintendents struggle to make things work with $10,000 per pupil, think how difficult it must be for the adult education administrators who must make it work with $800 per pupil. Simply put, they can't make it work. As a result, fewer than 10 percent of the people who need adult education services can access them.

And yet, we often hear people say, "Education is the key to success." What happens to those individuals who can't make it in public school, drop out, and can't access an adult education program because they are part of the 68 percent of those who need services but are on a waiting list? Or they can't access an adult education program, because the only available program is located too far from where they live? These people become the unemployed. They use tax-supported resources. Many become involved in the criminal justice system.

It's not a good thing when most of our society doesn't realize $225 billion in potential tax revenues are lost each year due to low literacy and numeracy. This information needs to be broadcast far and wide. If people were aware, they might choose to influence their legislatures to mitigate this with the provision of more resources. These additional resources could enable people to successfully access services to complete a high

---

5 Adult Literacy Facts. (2018) Available at: https://proliteracy.org/Resources/Adult-Literacy-Facts

school credential. To prove a point, if we divided $225 billion equally across 50 states, each of our state legislatures would have an extra $4.5 billion in the budget.

If we would invest tax dollars on the front end and provide the funding needed to educate our citizens, we wouldn't have as much lost tax revenue from unemployment. We wouldn't be spending as much money on incarceration. Educated people get jobs. They are productive citizens. They contribute.

As it stands, we can't figure out how to invest more than $800 per adult learner, or $10,000 per K–12 student, but we don't know about the $225 billion lost every year to low literacy and numeracy among our citizens. As a society, what do we value?

## Chapter 5

# THE IMPACT OF POVERTY

Education is the pathway out of poverty. Outside of my normal, students come from homes where adults are uneducated and unemployed. If the adults are employed, they are barely making enough money to pay for food or essentials. Those who are living within the law often work more than one job to make ends meet, leaving them little time to care for their children. Once again, the circumstances cause children to spend much of their time with little adult supervision or intervention outside of school.

School is not a comfortable place for uneducated adults living in poverty. They weren't successful in school. They don't have good memories of school. Some feel marginalized. In fact, it is much easier for a parent to make a scene in the school office than it is to acknowledge how uncomfortable he feels in a place where he thinks the other adults treat him like they are better than he is.

People who live in poverty reside in neighborhoods that keep them from getting ahead. Business owners in these neighborhoods struggle to find employees who are qualified. These neighborhoods are often magnets for crime, and people don't feel safe; businesses are often unsustainable.

For those without jobs, unemployment systems make it more profitable to stay unemployed than to seek work at all. If a person manages to pick up an odd job to earn a little income during a week of unemployment, he can't collect an unemployment subsidy. The truth is, he needs both. As a result, people ask to be paid in cash so there is no record, and then they can also claim the unemployment subsidy; or worse, they often give up on unemployment subsidies and find a new source of income through drug dealing or other criminal activity.

Not long ago, I attended a conference where the keynote speaker remarked that equity for all was not the same as equal access. As I pondered the meaning of this, I came back to the idea of making sure everyone has a level playing field. All little children can start school when they are five years old, but each brings a different normal to the classroom, and this impacts their ability to learn. Those children who come from poverty don't understand our normal or why they have to fit the mold of someone else's norms. As a result, they don't always behave the way we would expect them to behave. They aren't always able to achieve at the same level as their peers. Children in poverty are worried about their basic needs, not whether they can read or do math. For them, school is a place where they can get breakfast and lunch.

Eventually, they decide it is easier to stay home and escape the failure of school. After all, their parents didn't finish school. It's normal.

## Chapter 6
# THE SCHOOL TO PRISON PIPELINE

When I think about the word "pipeline," I picture something carrying a substance from one point to another. The water pipeline under my street carries the water from the treatment plant to my house. In my experience as a school administrator in the juvenile justice space, I heard the phrase "school to prison pipeline," and it took me a while to understand its meaning. Once I did, it made me pause.

Picture a pipeline large enough for youth to walk from Point A to Point B. They enter at Point A, which is the school door. Point B is the door to incarceration.

Those students who drop out of school exit the school door. They take to the streets, staying away from the adults in their homes, looking for something but not knowing exactly what. It doesn't take long before they follow the pipeline to Point B.

Maybe they don't drop out of school. They might be caught with drugs or drug paraphernalia on school property. Or they might have something in their possession that can be used as a weapon. Because of zero tolerance policies prevalent in schools, they are expelled. These students, some with criminal charges against them, are sent away to the local juvenile detention center to await the disposition of their cases.

Many of these students are children of color, children in poverty, children of an incarcerated parent, and children identified for special education services. Typically, these young people have not been attending school on a consistent basis, are well behind their peers academically, and generally aren't identified as achievers in school. Although their school administrators would never admit it publicly, to see these youth disappear from their attendance rosters is a relief for many reasons, not least of all because they are no longer part of the school's accountability measures.

However, although many people don't realize it, there are schools inside juvenile detention centers and correctional facilities. As a public school teacher, it never occurred to me. Just as I soon forgot about my student who murdered her mother and left a vacant seat in my vocal music class, most of these children are out of sight and out of mind. They break the law, disappear from school, and fade from memory.

I taught in one of these juvenile schools for four years after having taught in public schools for 17 years. When I first arrived to teach at the juvenile school, I was surprised the students only went to school for half the day. Half of the facility's population attended school in the morning, and the other half attended school in the afternoon. On Wednesdays, school was closed so teachers could participate in treatment team meetings. At these meetings, each student's overall progress in the program was documented, and a determination was made about when he would be released.

No school on Wednesdays. And yet, state and federal law states these youth must be in school, every day, all day. They were supposed to be taking the same courses that they would be taking if they were enrolled in school in their communities. More specifically, in Indiana, the law states high school students must have six hours of instruction per day, five days per week.[6] The students at this juvenile school received two and a half hours of instruction per day, four days per week.

Over the years, I found those who are incarcerated in juvenile facilities have similar characteristics when it comes to their academic achievement. Typically, about two-thirds of them test below the sixth grade in reading and math. A disproportionate number are identified to receive special education services; most qualify for services under the categories of *emotional disability* or *specific learning disability*. They haven't been successful in school, and most are convinced they will never be successful in school. The youth at the juvenile school where I taught were no exception.

---

6 Available at: https://www.doe.in.gov/accountability

Stop. Pause. Consider. They often read and do math below the sixth-grade level, but they must take the courses they would be taking if they were enrolled in school in their communities. High school courses. Algebra. Biology. Earth Science. World History. English. Electives.

At this school of about 300 students, over 60 percent were identified to receive special education services. I was one of four licensed special education teachers. One of these teachers was responsible for coordinating all the special education services, including the development of each student's individualized education program during a case conference with the parents, so she was not assigned to teach in a classroom. That left three licensed special education teachers to address the needs of 180 students who qualified for special education services. Although there were a handful of other teachers with emergency certification in special education, none of them were taking the courses to obtain the license.

I went into the school's office on my first day and asked about getting a lesson plan book. The principal looked at me and said there weren't any lesson plan books, but I could probably buy one somewhere. He showed me where the supply room was, and I managed to find a gradebook, some loose-leaf paper, and some pencils to use in my classroom.

When I got to my classroom, I noticed the textbooks on the bookshelves were outdated. The classroom floor was filthy, and the desktops had writing all over them. I asked around to see about getting the floor cleaned, and I was told the school did not have maintenance staff. There were mops and buckets in the closet at the end of the hall for me to use. Or, if I wanted, I could wait until the afternoon when some of the boys who were teacher aides could assist me. I'm not averse to cleaning my own room. My point is when I taught in public schools, we had a maintenance staff and custodians who kept our schools clean and ready. Here, if the teachers and students wanted to have a clean classroom, they had to do it themselves.

I wasn't allowed to be alone with students until I had completed all my Department of Correction training, so I observed other teachers in their classrooms. The typical class began with the teacher distributing folders and textbooks to the students. The folders contained lists of assignments they had to work through to complete the chapters in the textbook. Then the students would take the test for each chapter. After they completed all the chapters, they would earn their credit for the course. There was little large-group instruction or discussion, and the teacher would sit behind the desk, doing anything but teaching. New students came in each week and others left, making it difficult for them to plan large-group instruction…so they said.

My new colleagues talked about how great it was to teach inside a prison, because they didn't have to communicate with parents. One told me, "These students aren't really expected to learn anything, so it doesn't really matter what you do with them." Another told me the students weren't capable of learning. It wasn't unusual to walk past a classroom and see students asleep at their desks, while the rest were watching a movie…not an educational video, but a movie found at Blockbuster.

In this juvenile facility, students attended school year-round, with the school closing only on holidays. Unlike public schools, there was no spring break, summer break, or Christmas break. The facility was part of a state agency, so when the state government closed for a holiday, the school closed, too. At the time, there were no report cards, no progress reports, and student transcripts were printed from an archaic computer listing course titles not aligned to the state's requirements for a high school diploma.

The fact that something as basic as a lesson plan was not important to those in charge of the school was shameless. Having another professional educator tell me he couldn't teach the students, because they weren't capable of learning was alarming. These students were not easy to motivate but of course they could learn. I would leave at the end of the day and think, *What if this were my child, locked up in a facility, attending a school like this?* The adults were apathetic. They didn't accept their responsibilities to meet the educational needs of the youth who were sitting in their classrooms day after day. I would soon learn my perspective was far different from theirs, because I came from teaching in a public school. My new colleagues weren't bad people. It was their normal.

After about a month of teaching in the juvenile school, I decided to go back to school and get licensed in school administration. I wanted to be in a position where I could effect change. Little did I know how soon I would get the opportunity to do it. I completed my license in 2004. By spring of 2005, I was selected to be the Director of Juvenile Education for our agency, with the responsibility of providing system-wide administrative oversight to the nine schools inside our juvenile correctional facilities across the state of Indiana.

A few months later, in the fall of 2005, Indiana received notice from the US Department of Justice (DOJ) regarding findings specific to the mental health, safety, and education of the youth in our care. Indiana entered into a settlement agreement with the DOJ, and it became apparent the focus of my job would center on bringing our agency into compliance with the DOJ settlement agreement. I thought of an expression my mother used to always use. When someone had to learn how to do something by going through difficulty, she would say "he experienced baptism by fire." Looking back at the five-year journey to compliance, that's exactly what it was.

*Chapter 7*

# FITTING A ROUND PEG INTO A SQUARE HOLE

When I began my career with the Indiana Department of Correction (IDOC) in 2001, the number of students incarcerated across nine state juvenile facilities (two female facilities, seven male facilities) approached 1,600. By law, youth could be kept in a juvenile facility until the day before they became 22 years old. In practice, there were youth as young as 12, but rarely were youth kept through age 22. That being said, there were many who were over the age of 18.

The typical youth incarcerated with IDOC was required to complete a leveled program. As he worked through the program, he would move from Level 1 to Level 4. Depending on how well he participated, completed his treatment assignments, and met his treatment, behavior, and school goals, he could finish his program in under a year. However, youth who didn't meet their objectives didn't move up a level, and this caused them to stay longer.

Other youth came to us with determinate sentences in which a judge would order them to be in our care for a particular amount of time. One example was a 14-year-old youth who killed his stepfather in a domestic disturbance in his home. He was ordered to stay with us through the age of 21. This youth was difficult to motivate. Most who came to us with determinate sentences exhibited the same apathy and discouragement, because it didn't matter if they worked hard in their treatment programs. They had to stay whether they completed their goals or not.

In 2005, our IDOC commissioner began to reduce our juvenile population. It became unusual for a youth to stay past the age of 18. Even then, 18-year-olds with 12-year-olds was quite an age spread. However, over time, our youth population decreased. At the time we started addressing all the citations made by the DOJ, we were down to six facilities from nine.

While the DOJ was focused on only two of the six facilities, Indiana wanted system-wide resolution to the issues. It would be necessary to bring all six schools into compliance. One of the elements of the settlement agreement required all certified teachers in our juvenile facility schools, as a condition of employment, to obtain additional licensure in special education. The objective of the state and the DOJ was to make sure there were enough teachers certified in special education since such a high percentage of our youth qualified for special education services. There was no way to choose which teachers would be required to go back and get their special education licenses, so the state decided to make it a system-wide requirement. I was the central office administrator who had to go to the schools on a regular basis and interact with teachers who were not happy with this new requirement, and because of their unhappiness, it was a challenge to move forward with other needed changes.

Students in public schools go to math class where a licensed math teacher teaches math and a licensed English teacher teaches English. The school is led by a licensed school principal, and the district is led by a licensed school superintendent. We generally take this for granted. And, if a child was struggling with math and we found out his teacher was not a licensed math teacher, we would probably step up and register a complaint about it. After all, how can our children be expected to learn math if the teacher wasn't qualified to teach it?

Our public schools are expected to follow state and federal law regarding student achievement and curricular offerings. Across the country, states have agencies specifically designated to provide oversight to school corporations regarding these laws. The agency develops and implements policy regarding teacher licensing, the provision of special education services, curriculum, and everything else specifically mandated to schools.

Yet, there are schools in juvenile justice settings where accountability is often overlooked. For example, since many of the youth in our facilities had low literacy levels, it was common for our state agency to hire elementary-certified teachers to teach them, even though the youths' age-appropriate grade level was junior high and high school. It was not unusual for these elementary-certified teachers to award high school math or English credits, because they happened to be teaching English or math to the students. Were these teachers wrong for doing this? Of course not. It was how things were done. Until the DOJ came around, no one had really paid attention. After all, these youth were incarcerated. At the very least, these teachers could be congratulated for trying to close the students' achievement gaps.

As parents, most of us have never had to question whether the courses on our child's high school schedule would qualify him for graduation. Our children registered for classes and got a class schedule, and we assumed everything on the schedule applied to a high school diploma. This was not the case in our juvenile schools; frankly, this was not the case in most juvenile jurisdictions across the country. As part of the DOJ settlement, we needed to make sure all the courses we offered were aligned to the state academic standards, so the courses met the requirements of the state's high school diploma. Much effort was involved in aligning our curriculum to the state's academic standards. Simply put, we needed to make our juvenile schools real schools.

When you examine the school transcript of a student from a public school, you will see an indication she is attending an accredited institution. However, when our students returned to public school after they left us, they carried with them a questionable transcript. Often, the receiving school officials would not accept credits from our schools, because we were not state accredited. When I investigated this, I discovered our schools could never be state accredited because our agency was not a legal school corporation. In order to be viewed as legitimate schools with viable high school credits, we sought accreditation through an international accrediting body AdvancEd, under the category of Comprehensive Special Purpose Schools. Although we couldn't get state accreditation through our Department of Education, we could get accreditation from a body recognized by our state's public schools. By obtaining AdvancEd accreditation, getting our curricula aligned to the state's academic standards and courses aligned to the state's high school diploma, we were able to mitigate the questions around whether the credits we issued were valid.

There is, however, one other important element to earning a high school credit. In public schools, students go to school, attend algebra class, do homework, and take quizzes and tests through the entire semester. They come to a point where the semester ends and grades for the course are issued. The grades and the corresponding high school credit become part of the student's transcript. Parents don't need to ask whether the teacher is teaching content and concepts aligned to the academic standards for algebra. Parents don't have to look for proof their child was taught everything he needed to know to get credit in algebra. They assume all those days in class, time spent doing homework, and all those quizzes and tests constituted the instruction and evaluation necessary to say without a doubt he had experienced all he needed to earn the algebra credit.

If someone had a question about the validity of the credit and wanted to investigate, the algebra teacher would pull out his lesson plan book and reveal all had been done over the course of the semester. The plan book would reveal a record of the instruction provided, the assignments, the quizzes, etc. and demonstrate indeed, the algebra credit was valid.

This scenario was not so in many schools in juvenile justice settings, including ours back in 2005. There were teachers in our schools who did not write lesson plans, did not have any kind of record of instruction they had provided, and could not show what it was the student had done to earn the awarded credit. For some teachers, if the student was in class for a specific number of days, he was passed on to another class and a credit was awarded. For others, if the student had completed a list of assignments and passed the chapter tests, a credit was awarded. There was nothing to document a student qualifying for special education services had received any specialized instruction, accommodations, or curriculum modifications. There was nothing to show that each of the academic standards for the course had been part of the instruction provided by the teacher.

Lesson planning is a basic requirement in a school, and the principal should check to make sure it is happening. Were these teachers evil or bad? Of course not. At the time, it was their normal, and no one had challenged it. No one had challenged it because, once again, the youth in these schools are not viewed as students in a school, but juveniles incarcerated in a correctional facility. School is not their primary reason for being there. They are adjudicated delinquents.

*Chapter 8*

# WHO PAYS FOR IT?

As we continued to work on bringing our schools into compliance, a big issue continually manifested itself: who pays for it? In many jurisdictions, there are arguments about who is responsible for the provision of education services to youth who are incarcerated. Is it the school district's responsibility? Is it the state's department of education that bears the responsibility? Is it the responsibility of the agency where the youth is incarcerated?

Peeling back the layers and educating myself and others about the wacky way we try to pay for school inside a juvenile correctional facility took much of my time and energy. I worked in an agency responsible for public safety.

This agency was not made up of educators and school administrators who understood schools and school funding. What's more, this agency was funded to advance its primary mission of promoting public safety, not educating youth. It was difficult at best to get funding for the things we needed. Naturally, I had to get in line with other division directors in our agency who needed things.

We had an average of 34 percent of our youth qualified for special education services, compared to the 15.4 percent average across the state in public schools. And two thirds of our youth tested below sixth grade in math and reading, even though they were enrolled in high school. It could be argued that some of the neediest youth in the state had the fewest resources available to educate them. Yet, I knew that any additional resources would be difficult to procure.

Our agency, funded by the state legislature, had a central budget that allocated specific amounts to each of its adult and juvenile correctional facilities to operate. Each facility's budget had to pay for the physical building, the staff, the food, the medical care, the clothes for the residents, etc. At the time, our agency had over 28,000 adults who were incarcerated and under 1,000 youth. The daily per diem for youth was a lot higher than adults because of so many legal requirements involved with youth, including school.

The state's budget agency contended our agency was funded through the legislature as a state agency and was not entitled to school funding through the state's school funding formula. Our agency contended it wasn't resourced to meet all the education mandates under the law. Whenever I had to approach our agency's fiscal staff with a need, I knew it would be tough if the need included the use of state funding.

One example of this was when the DOJ continued to cite us because we did not have a licensed school principal at one of our schools. In a public school, the situation could have been easily remedied by transferring someone from across town to be the principal of the school in question. However, our schools were spread across the state. Asking someone to transfer would mean asking him to relocate to another city.

Back in 2005, there was a hiring freeze for state employees, agency budgets were closely scrutinized, and it was not easy to secure funding for the things needing to be procured. Before we could post the position and hire a principal, we had to submit it for approval by the hiring freeze committee of our state's personnel department. The process included writing a justification for the need to create the position, post it, and fill it. The hiring freeze committee met once per week.

Even though our schools were being monitored and the state had entered into a settlement agreement with the US Department of Justice, it took over six months to get approval to hire a principal. I had to explain to the committee why we couldn't move someone into the position (there was no qualified person at the facility with the correct license), I had to justify why we needed to have a licensed principal to lead the school, and I had to wait for someone to determine where the money to fund the principal's salary was going to come from within the agency's budget.

In contrast, if there was a vacant principal's position in a public school, it would be filled in a timely manner.

Likewise, our DOJ-monitored school needed a licensed math teacher. At the time, there were approximately 130 students at the school and eight teachers, equating to about 16 students per teacher. State Personnel staff asked why I needed to hire another teacher when the existing teacher to student ratio was only 1:16. It became obvious to me that I was trying to frame the need based on a paradigm in which all teachers would be licensed to teach the content they were teaching. In the past, this wasn't one of the criteria used to hire teachers, so the people on the hiring freeze committee couldn't understand why I was making the request. I assumed they understood my perspective when they didn't.

I reframed my request using elements of the NCLB Act and the need for our agency to assign Highly Qualified (as defined by NCLB) staff to teach core academic subjects. As with the principal vacancy, it took several months to get permission to hire a math teacher to teach math to our students.

In a public school, I would not need to justify why we needed to hire a math teacher to teach math.

Even though our students went to school and had to be provided with the same opportunities as their peers in the community, most people didn't consider them students. They were youth who were incarcerated. Our schools weren't part of a school corporation. They were the responsibility of our state agency. The Department of Education had an entire state full of K–12 students to consider. Our incarcerated youth were not on the radar, and the Department of Education couldn't fund us like public schools anyway, since our agency was already funded. No part of Indiana's school funding formula would be attributed to students in our care.

As I went back and forth between agencies, trying to see if there was a solution to the issues surrounding school funding, it became clear that I wasn't in a position with the authority to effect a change. The law needed to be changed, delineating how education for our incarcerated youth would be funded. And, frankly, we need to be funded differently than a public school corporation. Our students attended school 260 days per year, not 185 to 190, like students in traditional schools. These extra days made our costs more than those of a public school. Our teachers were paid for 260 days, not 185 to 190. Our teachers were required to be dually licensed in a content area and special education, which meant many of them had graduate degrees, qualifying them for a higher base salary. Personnel costs alone took up much of our agency's juvenile facility budget allocations.

To this day, Indiana, like other states, needs to look at how it funds education for youth who are incarcerated. During the Obama administration, the US Department of Justice and the US Department of Education issued a joint statement specifying the responsibilities of state agencies to collaborate in the provision of education services to these youth.[7] Although an important first step, this joint statement

---

7 Available at: https://www2.ed.gov/policy/gen/guid/correctional-education/cr-letter.pdf

did not include any type of accountability for states to overhaul existing dysfunctional practices. We need to put things in place for every student to succeed, just as the federal law stipulates.

In order to do this, states need to assign their state departments of education the responsibility of providing oversight to the education of all students, including youth who are court-involved. This needs to be clearly delineated. Likewise, agencies responsible for youth who are in the juvenile justice system need to follow the education requirements outlined in state and federal law, as monitored by the state's department of education.

Youth in the juvenile justice system need to attend school for the same amount of time as their public school counterparts, and the education of these youth needs to be funded by the state's legislature using a version of the state's school funding formula, which includes the number of days in the extended school calendar, the percentage of youth identified for special education, and the number of youths enrolled in the school.

Additionally, supplemental funding through Title I, Part D, Subpart 1 (for state agencies) and Subpart 2 (for local school districts supporting a juvenile justice placement) needs to be in place. Supplemental funding through the Individuals with Disabilities Education Act (IDEA) Part B needs to be allocated to these youth based on the percentage of enrolled students identified for special education services, not the number of students enrolled.

States without any explicit law detailing the funding, operation, oversight, and provision of education services to youth under the age of 18 who are court-involved need to address this immediately. Legislators need to gather input from judges, public school administrators, juvenile detention administrators, correctional education staff, and juvenile correctional administrators. All who are involved need to take out a blank sheet of paper and design a model that meets the needs of these students; fitting a square peg into a round hole does not work.

Our society cannot wait another minute to do the right thing. Shrugging our shoulders and saying we can't do it reflects we don't care about an entire segment of our population. And then, who pays for it? We all do.

## Chapter 9

# CAN THESE YOUTH BE TAUGHT?

It is probably safe to say most of us don't like doing busy work. We don't like doing work that is valued for nothing. However, in our juvenile schools in 2005, it was not uncommon for me to see students doing worksheets and puzzles with no connection to course content or classroom instruction. It is disrespectful to ask someone to do busywork. It sends the message that a person and his time are not important enough to be valued.

As I spent time in juvenile schools, I also saw teachers hand students packets of worksheets and tell them to sit down, shut up, and do their work. No instruction or guidance was provided. No talking was allowed. I observed an adult who repeatedly returned an assignment to a student, with no additional guidance, expecting him to somehow get the correct responses. And yet, it wasn't good enough until it was 100 percent correct.

How do you think this plays out? Predictably, the students don't do the assignments. They put their heads down and sleep, giving up in frustration, or they act out and get removed from the classroom, which causes them more problems. Yet we as adults say it is their fault. They need to do what they are told. They need to do their work. They need to behave. Yet, I noticed if they put their heads down and slept, no one seemed to care. At least they weren't disturbing anyone. This was a miscommunication of expectations. Did we want the students to participate in class and complete their assignments? Or did we want them to leave everyone else alone?

A couple of months ago, I talked with some youth who were incarcerated in a juvenile detention center in another state. I asked them what made them want to learn. The responses were, "I learn what interests me," and "I have to want to know about it." One student said, "It makes it easier to focus when I work with someone." Another student remarked, "I don't like it when we read the same books we read in elementary school. I like to read new stuff."

I think back to all the times as a teacher when I heard students ask the question, "Why do we have to do this?" or "Is this for a grade?" I remember asking the same question myself when I was in school. Basically, they are asking, "What's the point of this?" It is a fair question. If the teacher can't respond satisfactorily, he might as well expect mediocre work from his students. The bottom line is we all want to do things relevant to us. We want our time to mean something. Why would we expect these students to behave any differently than we would under similar circumstances? And yet, we do. Worse, if the students are incarcerated, we criminalize this normal behavior. They get into more trouble, because they aren't following the rules or aren't doing what they are told. When they get into trouble, they don't move through their program as quickly and they have to stay longer.

Another time, in a detention center in another state, I observed a teacher in a classroom where the topic of the discussion was the Gettysburg Address. There wasn't a single student in the classroom who had heard of the Gettysburg Address. Yet, most of us would think it was reasonable for the Gettysburg Address to be a topic of discussion in school. After all, it was a speech given by President Lincoln after a devastating battle that killed thousands and thousands of Americans. How does a teacher make something like this, which happened so long ago, relevant to a group of students of color, who are unconcerned about its importance? He begins by asking them about equality. He gets them to discuss issues linked to the Black Lives Matter movement. He gets them interested in something they could connect with…and then, he brings it back to President Lincoln, who eloquently advocated for equality in the Gettysburg Address. He gets them to read the speech together and leads them through the vocabulary in the speech. They begin searching for the meaning and try to determine which part of the text related to the Black Lives Matter movement. No one had his head down. No one was sleeping. The students asked questions. They discussed. They voiced opinions. They thought critically. They learned. They entered the room knowing nothing about the Gettysburg Address and left the room having learned about its relevance, even today.

Those students were assigned to that teacher because they had been identified for special education services. They were low-level readers, but they were learning and discussing high-level vocabulary and they understood it. I thought back to the student who said, "I have to want to know about it." Of course. Sometimes it takes a thoughtful adult to show him he wants to know about it.

A few months earlier, following the horrific mass shooting in Las Vegas, Nevada, I observed the same teacher leading the students in a discussion of gun control. After a brief introduction, he had the students read an article about gun control and then analyze the text, looking for statements of fact and opinion. As they systematically worked through the article, there was a lengthy discussion about one statement and whether it was a statement of fact or a statement of opinion. One student stepped out and made a solid argument even though the rest of the class disagreed. These students, like the rest of us, don't like to be wrong in front of each other. And yet, the topic was meaningful, so they forgot about being wrong and engaged in meaningful discussion as they analyzed the statements. Not only were they learning about how to distinguish between fact and opinion, but they were learning how to respect each other's perspectives and debate without fighting.

In our places of employment, most of us have projects to complete. We often collaborate and discuss the projects during meetings. We set goals and objectives. We work together in teams. We don't often have the directive to "sit down, shut up, and do our work." In fact, we often get guidance or direction regarding the work assignments we are given.

These students need opportunities to learn and practice collaboration and discussion. They need to practice setting goals and objectives and making lists of steps needed to get there. They need to practice giving and receiving guidance. The aforementioned are all workplace skills. If we tell students to sit in their desks and complete assignments without talking, asking questions, or receiving guidance, we aren't doing them any favors. We are not preparing them for the world of work. We aren't preparing them to think.

We can't expect our youth to automatically know how to behave in a pro-social manner. We have to teach them. We must give them opportunities to rehearse before expecting them to perform. Can these students be taught? Of course, they can be taught. Does it take effort and planning to make learning relevant? Yes. It certainly does.

*Chapter 10*

# TAKING TECHNOLOGY FOR GRANTED

The Indiana Office of Technology (IOT) is a state agency that is responsible for providing IT services to every other state agency, including the Department of Correction. Our state government leaders felt this was the most efficient and cost-effective way to manage IT services. Picture one agency with the sole responsibility of making sure all state employees had the technology necessary to do their jobs. As usual, it sounded reasonable. And, for the most part, it was reasonable. However, our IDOC was also operating schools in juvenile and adult correctional facilities, and of course each of our schools at the very least needed to have a computer lab. As typical for most state agencies, IOT staff members were extremely busy and resources were stretched as much as possible to stay within budgetary limits. It was one thing to make sure all state employees had what they needed to do their work; it was another to try to set up and maintain computer labs for students who were incarcerated. Although I was able to secure grant funding to purchase computer hardware and software for computer labs in each of our schools, it took over a year to get one lab of 12 computers operating in one of our schools.

Students in public schools get to use up-to-date technology. All the time, I read about public schools with smart boards in every classroom, mounted projectors allowing teachers to display content for students to view, multiple computer labs where students can use software to help them build their skills in a specific content area, or practice using software programs to create presentations, spreadsheets, and practice word processing. Students learn to write their own computer code and create content using a variety of media. I read about schools who have replaced textbooks with iPads or other devices with preloaded textbooks and supplemental content.

Teachers in public schools can easily pull up a YouTube video clip from the internet and use it with their students as a means of starting a discussion on a relevant topic. They can establish virtual relationships with other classrooms all around the world, and the students can communicate as they might when they become employees of nationwide companies, or even global companies. The internet has made the world a very small place, and teachers are able to bring the world to their students.

Although access to technology is improving for youth who are incarcerated, it is very rare for a youth who is incarcerated to have access to the internet. This is for fear he will use it for illegal purposes. Accessing the internet would mean the ability to post on social media, taunt victims, or engage in criminal activities such as drug trafficking, to name a few. Because of this lack of internet connectivity, our teachers face a daily challenge of not having the use of typical tools available to their public school counterparts.

As a school administrator, I explored many different avenues for providing digital content to our youth who were incarcerated. Our agency provided some limited funding, and I secured Title I funds to systematically purchase smart boards for each classroom in each of our schools. At least with the smart boards the teachers could access the digital content and project it for the students. It took several years for us to get to the point where each classroom had a smart board. But by then, it was time to begin replacing them with updated equipment.

Public schools have their own IT directors and IT staff who facilitate the installation of hardware and software and ensure that it remains operational. These staff members can readily troubleshoot issues and address them. In our situation, even if we had tech-savvy teachers who might know how to install something, they weren't allowed to do so because everything had to be done by IOT staff. We had to follow protocol. And any software we wanted to purchase had to be approved by IOT staff who had to network it across our schools. It was an incredibly lengthy process. There were so many days when I was frustrated about how we were mandated by law to provide the same educational experiences as public schools despite the fact that we didn't have the same resources.

I didn't think our students would ever be like their public school peers, carrying around iPads, Chromebooks, or laptops. The whole issue of internet connectivity would prevent this from happening. As I talked with colleagues around the country who were trying to convince their policy makers to allow internet connectivity, I was discouraged because I was not making any headway on the issue in Indiana. Understandably, no one wants to be in the news for facilitating criminal activity from inside a correctional facility. Couple this with the fear that someone would be connected to the state's network and might exploit it, there was no way I was going to be able to get permission for internet connectivity in our schools. Still, I kept thinking there had to be a secure way for our students to engage with digital content like their peers in public schools.

Months passed and then, within the same week, two trusted colleagues sent me a lead about a tech start-up called American Prison Data Systems (APDS). They told me I needed to get in touch with the cofounders of the company and explain what I was trying to accomplish with our students. Apparently, my colleagues had attended the same meeting in which they learned of the existence of this start-up, and they remembered I was searching for a secure device for our students to use. Independently of each other, they contacted me and told me about APDS and encouraged me to investigate the opportunity.

The months following my first contact with APDS were some of the most satisfying I spent in my 12 years as a statewide school administrator for incarcerated youth. The company itself is a Public Benefits Corporation, meaning it operated for profit, but also had a social mission. The social mission for APDS was to reduce recidivism through increased access to educational and treatment programming using secure devices. They weren't trying to replace teachers. They were helping us leverage technology to fill the gaps in our curriculum.

With APDS, we were able to initiate a small pilot program using the devices at one of our smallest schools. The devices worked using a separate, secure cellular connection. Students were not able to access the internet. All the content we wanted them to have would be sent through the cellular connection to the tablets. Our teachers would be able to put their own content on the devices using an app very much like Dropbox. I was excited when we received permission to give this a try. Our IOT staff members were satisfied the devices would not be connected to the state's network. Since they weren't, we were able to work with APDS to deploy the tablets without having to depend on the overworked IOT staff.

Like any new venture, there were some hiccups along the way, but there were no security breaches, and the best thing of all was our students loved their tablets. They read library books using the tablets. They did school work in the evenings and communicated with their counselors and teachers. They were able to listen to music, watch videos, and play games as rewards for good behavior. In this case, good behavior included the completion of assignments and participation in class.

We were able to use the tablets to provide everyone, even students who were in self-contained classrooms, with access to quality content including high school credit recovery and reading remediation. We saw reduced levels of grievances and fighting, because students used the tablets to interact with staff members and resolve issues before they became too difficult to manage. Students could choose to separate themselves from volatile situations by taking their tablets off to a corner and doing something productive.

When we first gave the devices to the students, some of the adults in the facility expressed concern. They thought we were rewarding students with something they didn't deserve. I reminded them of the need for our students to practice using the same types of technology their peers were using. Our students entered our schools far behind their age-appropriate peers when it came to academic achievement. To keep them from using similar technology and accessing the same types of content as their public school counterparts would merely cause them to lag behind more when they returned to their communities.

Word quickly spread, and staff in our other juvenile schools started asking when they were going to get tablets in their schools. I began the process of getting additional pricing from APDS, so we could expand tablet use into our other schools. I wanted to be able to provide digital content to all youth in our care. However, once again, our youth fell victim to the system: IDOC decided it wanted tablets for everyone, adult and juvenile, and of course the rules for such a significant purchase dictated the procurement needed to go out for bid. Our expansion of our small pilot was on hold. We would not be able to expand our use of APDS tablets to the other juvenile schools until the state determined which tablet vendor it wanted to use.

The statewide tablet procurement process started in 2015, and it took over two years for a vendor to be chosen. By that time, IDOC had made the decision to relocate the students and close the facility where the APDS tablets were in use. Our ability to amplify and supplement the instruction and programming through the use of the APDS devices became history.

## Chapter 11

# SCHOOL ACCOUNTABILITY: OUR NORMAL

Every public school corporation I have encountered has some type of Title I program. When I was teaching in a public elementary school, the federal funds from Title I were used for students who needed additional help with reading and math. The formal name for Title I is, "Improving the Academic Achievement of the Disadvantaged," and its purpose is to "ensure all children have a fair, equal, and significant opportunity to obtain a high-quality education, and reach, at a minimum, proficiency on challenging state academic achievement standards and state academic assessments."[8]

8 Title I—Improving the Academic Achievement of the Disadvantaged. (2018). Available at https://www2.ed.gov/policy/elsec/leg/esea02/pg1.html

Until I become the Director of Juvenile Education in Indiana, I didn't realize the Title I law included a specific section to address students who were neglected and delinquent. This section of the law, Title I, Part D, Subpart 1, became second nature to me and there were times I felt like I had it memorized.

If it weren't for these Title I funds, our juvenile schools would not have benefited from many of the tools taken for granted in a public school. Among other things, Title I, Part D, Subpart 1 funded equipment for computer labs, equipment for vocational programming, digital content for our APDS tablets, programming to provide reading remediation, and professional development for our teachers. Title I funded the development of a state-of-the-art student information system to assist teachers and administrators with data collection and analysis, consultants to work directly with our teachers and administrators, and staff to support student transition.

Student transition is a big deal with Title I, Part D, Subpart 1; so important that the law requires at least 15 percent, but not more than 30 percent of the grant funding be spent on transition-related activities. Of course, when federal funding is awarded, there is accountability associated with it. We had to submit annual data regarding the number of youth who re-enrolled in their public school after they were released from us, how many received a high school credential (GED, TASC, HiSET), how many received a high school diploma, how many enrolled in a post-secondary (college) program, how many had secured employment, and how many enrolled in a vocational (job training) program. The problem associated with this (for us, and for everyone else across the country who receives Title I, Part D, Subpart 1 funding) was we often knew what the youth had planned to do when they left us, but we couldn't always track what actually happened.

For example, we had a staff member in each school who would call the youth's intended high school to inquire if the youth had enrolled and to facilitate the transfer of his educational record. Often, we would find the youth was not enrolled. Perhaps he moved to a different school district. We had no way of knowing, and we had no way of determining which school he might have attended instead. As a result, we couldn't track him. Likewise, if there wasn't another public school expecting him to enroll, those school officials wouldn't be looking for him. He was in the wind.

Perhaps he was finished with school and his transition plan included getting a job. He might have even stated he was going to get a job with a specific employer. Our staff member couldn't call the employer to verify this. A follow-up phone call would reveal previous incarceration and could prejudice the employer against the youth.

Although our schools weren't state accredited, we were connected and accountable to Indiana's Department of Education through Title I, Part D, Subpart 1 and through IDEA Part B (Special Education) funding allocations. We also had to report our data to the Indiana Department of Education just as any public school, and we had to make sure we provided our students with the opportunity to participate in the state's mandated standardized testing.

Between 2005 and 2017, Indiana's overall standardized assessment processes evolved like every other state. During this time, K–12 students went from paper-pencil testing to computer-based testing. As previously noted, computer-based testing was a problem for us. However, between 2005 and 2017 the total enrollment on any given day in our juvenile correctional facility schools went from approximately 1,500 students in nine facilities to 400 students in three facilities. When considering the impact of designing a standardized testing process for the entire state, 400 students shouldn't factor into the decision about whether or not to utilize technology when conducting assessments. Still, there were 400 students who needed to take the assessments, like any other student in the state, so there needed to be an alternative option for them.

Here's an example of how the alternative option looked. At one time in Indiana, it was required that a student pass the state's standardized End of Course Assessment (ECA) in algebra in order to be eligible to receive a high school diploma. That meant the student not only had to have a high school credit in algebra, but he had to pass the state's standardized test. The state offered computer-based ECA testing many times during the year, so students could take the test as soon as they completed the algebra credit. However, paper-pencil ECA testing was only offered twice per year.

The impact of this was our students often completed a high school credit in algebra but had no way to take the ECA, because the testing window for paper-pencil assessment didn't occur while they were with us. This caused them to have to wait to take the standardized assessment upon re-enrollment at a public school. Or, they may have completed algebra with us but had to wait several months for the paper-pencil testing window, so they could complete the ECA with us. The alternative option for our students was actually a barrier. Waiting an extended time to take a mandated standardized assessment after completing a course made it very difficult for our students to be successful. In this instance, the barrier had the potential of keeping the student from graduating from high school.

## Chapter 12

# JAG AND AVID: TWO INITIATIVES TO KEEP YOUTH IN SCHOOL

Jobs for America's Graduates (JAG) is a state-based, national nonprofit organization whose primary mission is preventing our at-risk youth from dropping out of high school. The best way to prevent youth from going deep into the system is to keep them in school. I have become a huge fan of JAG. Our governor brought JAG to Indiana in 2006. Since then, it has expanded into 135 sites across our state.

Think about the youth who might be considered at-risk for becoming high school dropouts. Remember, these are the youth who might come from poverty. They might come from homes where the adults are not supervising them or providing for them. They might come from homes where the adults are uneducated, unemployed, or both. Struggling with learning or dealing with so many other life issues would often put school attendance on the low priority list. They come from situations much like the students enrolled in our juvenile justice schools. Luckily, they haven't gotten far into the system yet.

Students who are enrolled in JAG programs get to experience daily adult mentoring during their time in school and for one year after graduation. They participate in work-based learning experiences, visit college campuses, and have guidance completing the Free Application for Federal Student Aid for post-secondary education. Students enrolled in JAG meet together every day. JAG isn't taught by a licensed teacher, but facilitated by a JAG specialist, who is a caring adult mentor.

Students in JAG are guided through career exploration and goal setting. They are taught essential skills necessary to be successful adults, such as working with others, dependability, accountability, respect, trustworthiness, and leadership. These essential skills, which transcend post-secondary settings, employment settings, and life settings, are acquired through participation in a variety of classroom and community activities that allow them to practice and gain confidence.

For example, in Indiana, each JAG program sponsors annual competitions that include categories such as public speaking, writing skills, career presentations, financial literacy, creative solutions, critical thinking, entrepreneurship, and employability skills. Youth engage in local competitions and have the opportunity to advance to regional competitions. Eventually, they participate in a state competition, where they spend the day on the community college campus, interacting with their peers from around the state, and receiving recognition for their achievements.

For three years, I was privileged to participate as a judge for the state competition. I had the opportunity to interview each of 12 regions' Outstanding Senior candidates. The process involved reading each student's application, which included an essay often interspersed with pieces of their personal stories. After that, I was part of an interview panel that met with each student personally. Following the first year of participating in the Outstanding Senior interviews, I learned to bring a box of tissues to the interview room. As the youths spoke about their experiences, it wasn't unusual for them to become teary, along with everyone else in the room. So many of them had very touching stories. Every single one of these students spoke of their JAG family and the fact they would not have been successful in high school had it not been for their JAG specialist.

How successful is JAG? In Indiana, approximately 95 percent of JAG participants graduate from high school. Many of Indiana's JAG specialists and program management staff members have received national recognition. I attended one of JAG's national events in which the keynote speaker was a JAG student from Indiana. Another student at this same event spoke of her life before JAG. She likened herself to a penny on the sidewalk, waiting for someone to care enough to stop and pick her up.

This successful program was born out of the need to prevent high school dropouts, so the nation's workforce could be positively impacted. In Indiana, JAG is supported with limited federal Workforce Innovation and Opportunity Act funds, and the legislature has funded the Indiana Department of Workforce Development budget to support ongoing expansion of the program throughout the state. It is not an education initiative. It is a workforce initiative.

JAG students found success when they connected to adults and peers who became like family. They needed an adult to be there for them every day, encouraging them to persevere through the tough days and celebrating successes with them along the way. They needed a place physically and emotionally safe for them to be themselves. Based on the many stories given by JAG students, it was JAG that gave them hope and showed them that their normal wasn't the only normal out there.

JAG is a program designed for students in high school. For some, high school is too late for intervention. Those students who experience school failure at a younger age might not make it to high school JAG programs, where they can connect with caring adult mentors. For some, if the intervention doesn't come at an earlier point in their lives, they drop out.

One program that intervenes at an earlier state is AVID, or Advancement Via Individual Determination. AVID has a slightly different approach than JAG. For one thing, AVID is an education initiative, not a workforce initiative. We know students at-risk for dropping out of school come from a variety of socio-economic backgrounds, cultures, and environments. AVID encourages teachers to recognize the diverse environments and cultures from which they come and shift the way they do things, so every student can engage.

You might think, "Well, of course! Teachers should recognize all students don't learn the same way." We often hear we parent the way we were parented. Many teachers teach the way they were taught. And they come from a different normal than many of the students in their classrooms. It isn't always easy to recognize what is behind a student's inability to be successful. Multiply that by 20 other students in a classroom, each with his own set of circumstances, and a teacher truly has her job cut out for her.

The AVID model includes professional development for teachers who then become the catalyst for systemic change in their schools. AVID is a very comprehensive initiative. Schools who use AVID rely on instructors and administrators who have received AVID training. Students enrolled in classrooms with AVID-trained teachers still experience the same rigor and high expectations as their peers, but they are instructed in a manner that meets their needs and allows them to achieve success.

Both JAG and AVID guide students with goal setting. They provide students with hope and set them on a more positive life trajectory. They encourage adults to peel back the layers until they get to the essence of the person behind the face, and then meet the person's need. They help our most needy youth become resilient.

## Chapter 13
# ANY HOPE FOR RESILIENCE?

Resilience is defined as being able to recover quickly from difficulties or adversity. Some people are like that. They don't let difficulties or adversity define them. How is it some people are more resilient than others? Is there any hope for resiliency among members of this population who are up against so many barriers?

People with resilience are goal setters. They are planners. They look to the future with a sense of purpose. They are socially competent and able to develop positive relationships with others. At an early age, maybe as a means of survival, they develop a sense of self and navigate life autonomously. This sense of independence and self-determination manages to get them through difficult times.

Having these strengths of character doesn't guarantee resiliency. Life is hard. For one young woman, the adults in her life made a huge difference. I am changing her name to protect her, but her story is true.

Rose is a 20-something young woman whose father was addicted to drugs. Early in life, he committed a felony and was sent to prison, leaving her alone with her mother and older sibling throughout her elementary and middle school years. Her mother, who did not have a high school credential, was left to support the family. Rose was a good student. She managed to keep her father's incarceration to herself, because none of her peers ever really asked about her father. Twice a month, her mother would take her to visit him in prison. She remembers getting gifts from him at Christmastime through programs like Angel Tree.

Rose's father was released from prison around the time she started high school. His drug addiction continued, and there were times she would come home from school to find the family's television or other items gone, because he had taken them and sold them to get money for drugs. One time, he even invaded her room and took some of her personal belongings and sold them. He couldn't keep a job, and sometimes he would be gone for weeks at a time. Rose knew when he was gone, he was probably out running with his friends who were also doing drugs.

Despite the daily upheaval at home, she kept going, becoming the first in her family to finish high school, and earned a full scholarship to college. She decided to major in education and become a teacher.

In time, things at home settled down, her father found a job, and her family established a routine. By this time, Rose was off at college and didn't experience family life first-hand. She excelled in her studies and became the first in her family to earn a bachelors degree. Everyone was proud of Rose. She was a beautiful, talented, intelligent young woman. Rose was resilient.

How is it that Rose was able to succeed, even though by definition, she was an at-risk youth? When asked about this, Rose was very thoughtful. She described the times she would hang out at the home of her best friend and see a different picture of family life, which helped her realize there was hope for something different. She said when she was in middle school, one of her teachers took an interest in her and helped her set a goal to earn a college scholarship. Until that time, she hadn't even considered she would be able to go to college. This gave her hope for something different. On the day she came home from school and found her father had taken her special belongings and sold them for drugs, she was crushed. She said that as she wrote about it in her journal, she chose to hope for something different.

Rose said school was always a safe place for her. It was consistent. People cared for her. She was happy there.

For Rose, resiliency was the ability to cope and adapt. Watching others make mistakes and fail became helpful feedback to her as she chose to learn from their mistakes. Although some of the problems she faced were not solvable, she learned to manage them, because along the way she encountered circumstances that allowed her to hope for something different.

Now, Rose has a job teaching in a prison classroom. Her students have no idea that she is the daughter of an individual who was incarcerated. She understands addiction. She understands the problems and struggles that her students face, because she has lived through them herself. Her perspective makes it easy for her to relate to them and help them succeed. She strives to make her classroom a safe place for her students to learn. At the time of this writing, Rose's students successfully pass the high school equivalency exam with greater frequency than students from most other classrooms.

Rose's resilience and the way she has chosen to give back is remarkable. During her young life, she encountered adults who sparked inspiration and hope. She spent time with others and realized her normal didn't have to be static. She used this as a catalyst to set goals for herself. Once she achieved her goals, she returned to a place where she could provide similar inspiration and hope. She is an example of how caring adults can make a difference to a child's life trajectory.

## Chapter 14

# WILLFUL BARRIERS OR SIMPLE IGNORANCE?

Every time I would get discouraged about a particular barrier our youth encountered, or a barrier I encountered as I was advocating for them, I had to force myself to stop and analyze it. I had to choose to believe the barrier wasn't put there on purpose; it was the result of an unintended consequence or the result of someone's ignorance. After all, until I became immersed with educating youth in the justice system, I was ignorant about these issues as well.

For example, re-enrollment into public school after being incarcerated in a juvenile facility school was and continues to be a barrier, with no easy solutions if the system continues as it is. Students have the law on their side; they have the right to re-enroll in public schools and complete their high school diplomas. But most public school officials really don't want Johnny or Sally back in school, for reasons we have already discussed. Although they might have earned credits towards their diplomas and achieved academic successes while they were with us, they were still behind their age-appropriate peers, and the reality was they probably wouldn't graduate on time or would struggle with the statewide standardized assessment. Not to mention, they had left a school where people remembered them as difficult. For many, it took a lot of courage to even return to the school and seek to re-enroll. Some didn't even try.

From time to time, I would receive a phone call from a parent who was experiencing difficulty with re-enrolling the child. I would call the principal of the school and politely remind him that the student had a right to re-enroll and ask if he would like for me to send along the student's educational record. Certainly, the principal already knew this. Usually, it was a case where the principal or guidance counselor at the public school had tried persuading the youth to enroll in an alternative school or an adult education program, and the parent would think that the youth couldn't re-enroll. A simple phone call to the school was usually enough for the principal to take the parent more seriously the next time he was approached about re-enrolling the youth.

I often wondered, "What's so different about our students? What if this youth had never been incarcerated, but was a student who was simply moving into the district, with the same academic baggage? Would it be different?" I have to think the parents or guardians of our youth who have been incarcerated have become used to getting doors slammed in their faces. If they are told, "You can't do this," they believe it. They don't always know their rights, or their youth's rights, so they take it all at face value. No matter what encouragement they have received from us, all it takes is a negative response from someone in a position of authority and they step back. They have grown accustomed to negative responses.

During my last year in my role as school administrator with IDOC, I spent a great deal of time collaborating with the staff responsible for youth programming at the Indiana Department of Workforce Development. These were the same staff who were responsible for the oversight of programs like JAG. A common denominator for both of our agencies was the need to delineate clear pathways for youth to succeed. These pathways began with the completion of a high school credential, followed by postsecondary education, or job-certification training, followed by employment in a job providing sustainable wage leading to a desired career.

Through our collaboration, we decided to implement a different approach to transition. Instead of sending our youth directly back to their public schools to re-enroll, we started sending them to the DWD youth representative for their region. From there, the youth would work with the representative to determine the most advantageous path. Perhaps it was enrollment in an adult education program to finish a high school credential, or perhaps it was enrollment in a public school connected to a JAG program. It might be the youth already had a high school credential and could access training (at no cost to him) leading to entry-level certification in a job sector offering employment with a sustainable wage. In any case, this seemed to make more sense and was certainly worth a try. Collaboration with the workforce development agency instead of the public school seemed a little out of sync with the normal expectation, but at this point, I had learned normal was relative.

Making this change involved a lot of cross-training. Our teachers didn't naturally know about all the offerings available to youth through the DWD. Our teachers know education. We had to help them learn about these other options, so they could in turn teach our youth about them. Likewise, the DWD staff had to train its regional representatives about our youth and their needs so they knew what to expect when we connected our youth with them. This was new for DWD staff, who were used to employment pathways, not Title I, Part D, Subpart 1 transition requirements.

At the time of this writing, one year after implementing our new transition process, my successor is in the midst of reviewing data to determine if this change made a difference. Based on my experience, they will need to consistently train staff and adjust or improve processes, but this alternative to the traditional transition to school pathway seems to be a promising practice.

## Chapter 15
# MAKING IT FIT

Not long ago, my daughter sent me a video of my toddler granddaughter trying to fit differently shaped blocks into their corresponding openings in a container. She tried fitting the triangle into the square opening. She tried fitting it into the circle opening. She tried fitting it into the rectangle opening. Finally, she gave up, lifted the lid to the box, and tossed the triangle-shaped block inside the container. She didn't waste any more time trying to make it fit. She found a solution.

That video reminds me of what we accomplished inside our juvenile schools. A square peg can't fit into a round hole.

We couldn't make excuses. We needed to get things done. We had to shape our schools into the very best they could be with the resources we had available to us. No complaining about funding. No complaining about barriers. We had to figure it out.

That's what we have done. Our team made checklists from the list of DOJ citations, and we started working on them. We had to align our curriculum. We had to ensure all of our certified staff were given teaching assignments that were appropriate given their professional licensing. We had to bring our education policies and practices into compliance with state and federal laws. We had to improve instruction and transition practices while collecting and analyzing data. We had to facilitate the receipt and transfer of educational records. The list was long, but it was critical. Our students needed a quality education.

With the help of some fantastic professionals, we reformed our curriculum and acquired updated textbooks. We designed a lesson plan template that could be used by all teachers to reflect instruction that was aligned with the state's academic standards. Not only that, the lesson plans documented instructional accommodations for those students with special needs. We had a consultant who coached our teachers and showed them how they could engage students in the classroom using a variety of instructional strategies. We had a consultant who worked with our administrators and showed them how to collect data specific to instructional practices. Our administrators did a lot of classroom observations and collected a lot of objective data.

Our team was strong. We created a state-of-the-art system for collecting and analyzing student data. This Student Information Management System (SIMS), was nothing short of fantastic. Since its creation, people from around the country, along with staff at our Indiana Department of Education, have been treated to demonstrations of SIMS and have been extremely impressed with what it does and what we do with it.

Over the course of several years, we have managed to put together transition protocols that have garnered national recognition. These protocols involved a series of biweekly individual interviews between the teacher and each of the students on her caseload. These transition consultations led to the compilation of comprehensive transition plans for each student to follow at the time of release from our facility.

Our team forged relationships with many of the various program divisions within our state's Department of Education. Even though our schools weren't traditional, we finally reached the point where they were recognized as credible. New curriculum, instruction, and records reflected that students' time and effort in school was not wasted. Our accreditation through AdvancEd as Comprehensive Special Purpose Schools added to this credibility.

Even though our schools weren't part of a school corporation, we established our own accountability criteria and used objective data to measure our progress towards stated objectives set by each principal at the beginning of the school year. For example, we graded each school based on the percentage of special education students who made appropriate progress towards the goals on their individualized education plans. Since our students were not with us for an entire school year, we quantified each goal and tracked student progress. If the trend line towards completion was positive across the months the student was with us, our accountability criteria were met.

We also graded our schools based on how many students showed growth in reading and math while enrolled, how many students earned an appropriate number of high school credits, and how many age-appropriate youths earned a high school credential (either by completing the requirements for a diploma or successfully passing the high school equivalency exam). SIMS mined data on a daily basis and sent prompts to teachers regarding student progress. If a student's grades started to drop, the teacher was prompted to look carefully at the data to determine if the student needed additional supports or interventions. If a student received more than two failing grades in a class, the teacher was prompted to use or add an accommodation. We had a way to make sure every student's needs were addressed.

We wanted to make sure our accountability measures were rigorous, but reasonable. We didn't want standardized testing to be the focus. We wanted the focus to be student learning and positive student outcomes. Our students were difficult and brought many challenges to our classrooms. And yet, this was the last stop for them. If we couldn't help them achieve success, how could we provide them with any hope for a better future? We needed to be able to show them a different version of what their life could become. Success in school was paramount for achieving this outcome. We knew that if our students were uneducated, we would be sentencing them to a lifetime of unemployment, with all the negative consequences it entails.

Our students find it difficult to trust adults, because they have been let down by adults. They don't think about the future, because they can't see beyond the present. They can't see beyond the present, because they have spent so much of their lives in survival mode. Setting goals is foreign to them. Having hope is even more remote.

We began to embrace our responsibility of helping our youth make a realistic plan for their futures. The transition consultations gave our students the opportunity to talk about their career interests with a caring adult. They were able to think about their goals and what they would need to accomplish in order to reach those goals. Our students are teenagers, and like any other teenager, they need someone to help them think about where they want to go and the path that can take them there.

Every school can always improve. Yet, our team worked hard to provide our students and teachers with the resources they needed for teaching and learning. We value our students and are invested in their progress. We are the caring adults who can provide them with hope.

## Chapter 16
# IMAGINE THE POSSIBILITIES

What if this were my child? If my child had to attend one of our juvenile schools, would I be confident she was getting a quality education? Back in 2001, I would have said no. Today, I am more confident. Our staff does the best it can with the resources available. Even so, our juvenile schools still take a back seat to almost everything else in the state, at the expense of the youth who are required to attend them. By jumping ahead and shaping our schools into the best they could be with the resources available to us, we still never really solved the whole fitting a square peg into a round hole problem. Our youth continue to be considered incarcerated individuals in a correctional facility, not students attending school in a correctional facility.

The issues I have outlined and discussed in this book are not specific to Indiana. They are prevalent across the country. My colleagues in other states grappled with the very same problems we did; all of us continue to grapple with them. Why is it we can identify key issues, but we can't seem to solve them? Is it because they are truly unsolvable, or is it because the solution would cost too much money? At the risk of sounding jaded, I have come to believe that this population of youth is simply not valued. These youth are invisible. They are forgotten, surrounded by adults who have let them down and continue to let them down. Once they fall off the radar of their public schools, there is really no way to keep track of them.

Imagine what it could be like if our states funded education the way it needed to be funded and revised the ways we provide educational services in our communities. What if we had community centers within walking distance of those who lived there, and adult education programs were readily available at various times of the day, so our citizens could build a better future for themselves?

Imagine what it could be like if our K–12 schools had more social workers on-site, readily available to support those students who needed an extra one-on-one interaction from a caring adult. What if our school accountability plans actually incentivized those schools that re-enrolled at-risk students and helped them get across the finish line with a high school diploma, even if it took them a little extra time to complete it? I am encouraged by the fact that Indiana has developed new graduation pathways, which take effect with next year's (2019–2020) ninth-grade cohort. My hope is that the pathways will lead to success for all students, and those unintended consequences, which came about during the implementation of NCLB, won't create barriers for subgroups of students like those in the juvenile justice system.

Imagine what it would be like for school leaders to take real steps towards achieving solutions to the barriers impacting our children. I am encouraged the Indiana Department of Education recently hired an Assistant Director of Social, Emotional, and Behavioral Wellness. Indiana is one of only a few states taking the step to create a dedicated position for social and emotional learning. Recognizing the need to help schools address the impact of trauma on student learning and then doing something about it shows thoughtful leadership on the part of our State Superintendent of Public Instruction.

Imagine if we were able to compensate teachers and social workers as the valued professionals they are. These individuals are required to have professional licenses and most get graduate degrees. We entrust them with our most precious commodity (our children) and then ask them to accomplish much while respecting them very little. Educators and social workers are widely criticized about youth outcomes. Yet, they continue to go to school every day to do their very best to bring hope into the lives of those entrusted to them.

Imagine if we had an abundance of mental health professionals who could provide substance abuse treatment or other mental health services to youth and other family members in need. Imagine these mental health professionals providing services in locations close to schools or neighborhood community centers where they're easily accessible.

Imagine if we intervened proactively with children and their families, providing them with the social services they need so children could arrive at school, ready to learn.

Imagine if all jurisdictions needing secure technology had the means to purchase it and leverage it to provide education and treatment programming at no cost to those who needed it.

Imagine if we looked beyond the learner we see today and picture who he could become in the future. What if we treated him with basic dignity, even at his lowest point?

I understand all of this takes money. But what do we value? As a society, are we willing to continue to turn our heads and ignore the negative consequences of illiteracy and low numeracy? Are we willing to continue to spend more money on incarceration than education? Are we willing to be content with broken systems making it nearly impossible for youth to achieve any kind of success, let alone hope for anything better? We are the adults. We have a moral responsibility to those who have no control over what happens to them.

CPSIA information can be obtained
at www.ICGtesting.com
Printed in the USA
LVHW091922271118
598388LV00008B/197/P

9 781732 769410